Pieces of My Soul

By Kellie Fitzgerald

IbbiLane Press

ISBN 9798218178307 (paperback)

Front cover by Elizabeth Dunlap at Pixie Covers

Dedicated to love
and to all of us who still believe in it.

This book intentionally has no table of contents and no titles of individual writings. It's meant for you to find those words that speak to you, whatever it is you're going through at any given time, by simply opening the book to no specific page. Then you can give your own titles to what you find herein that moves your heart.

While it is acknowledged this is highly divergent it is the intent of the author and publisher that this collection of writings be "used" rather than simply "read." Thank you for indulging us.

She looks at the tears running down her
cheeks in the mirror
and smiles a sad smile.
"Isn't it funny how one single traumatic
event seems to unleash memories of all
the others that have ever happened?"
Then she sighed a deep sigh, planted a
smile on her face,
and readied herself for another day. It's
just what she does.

Watching another gorgeous sunset she
raises her glass to the sky
"I know you are out there, I can feel you.
If only I knew who you are."
Smiling to no one but herself she takes a
sip of her favorite wine
and toasts the unnamed person, while
sending love and peace to the planet
and to all those who feel unloved and
different,
like herself.

Night falls
and the faces of all those she loves
who are no longer on this side of the veil
fill the space in front of her face.

As stars fill the sky
she tries to hug each one of them
those faces belonging only
to her heart now

Tears stream
down her face and she doesn't notice
because she's lost in a dream
when the departed filled her life

Grief is a funny thing,
she says to herself
each time I think I've defeated the pain
I see the faces again

She loves simple things. A sunrise or a sunset. The smile of a stranger. The laughter of children at play or the joy of a dog chasing a ball. The wonderful things that make life worth living. But sometimes life is just not simple. Clouds close in and the sunrise and the sunset are hidden. Strangers don't smile, children aren't playing and there isn't a dog to be seen. Darkness closes in. She still loves those simple things though and she's realized they're still right there inside her heart and that even on those toughest days life is still worth living.

She stood on the precipice and waited for something, anything, to happen. At that moment it mattered not to her whether that something, anything, was good or bad. She had reached a dangerous point; she truly did not care what was happening around her anymore. She took a deep breath and gracefully stepped off the edge. As her wings opened she finally realized that she was so much more than they had allowed her to believe. Never again would she allow anyone to hold her down, for now, she soared.

Life isn't always pretty. Sometimes life is very ugly. Raw. Dark. Despondent. Sometimes life is anything except what we want it to be. Know that's OK. It's OK to be raw and dark and even despondent yourself sometimes. The darkness is where we often learn our most important lessons. Sometimes we need to peel back the pain and the hurt we feel. We need to become raw before we can heal. Some wounds are much deeper than others, much more severe. So feel however you feel. Only through feeling, really feeling, the pain can we heal it completely. While we often say don't let anyone take away your light, you shouldn't allow anyone to take away your darkness either. Your darkness is what will enable you to find your light again.

Life is a funny thing, she said, there's no point in making plans or striving to become something other that what you are because at the end of life you realize you were already whole and complete from the beginning.

My soul has known your soul for a
thousand years and more.
In the quiet moments of the day
when my mind is still
I feel you coming back into my life
this life, this timeline and
this dimension.
And I'm not sure what to feel,
But I feel your intensity of one
who is searching,
one who is in deep pain
and torment even.
Angels say I should stay open
for whatever the divine has ordered
and apparently the divine
has ordered you into my life
But I still have free will
and it is my final decision
that will say whether or not
we do this again
Still, my heart calls out to you
and my soul feels your familiarity
and at this moment
I do not know
what I will decide.

Meet me under the moon tonight
the way you always do
we'll stroll upon the milky way
and dance to our own tune.
I know I've always known you
and you have always known me
but this lifetime's been brutal
are we still meant to be?
So many important questions
with answers not to be found
but I hear angelic voices saying
keep the faith love's nearing now
And although my soul is weary
and my faith is wearing thin
I simply must move forward
my heart wants to try again.

3:36 in the morning
she is awakened by distant chanting
in a language she does not speak
but most certainly understands
the sound of drums
beating in a ceremonial way
beckon her to join them
and she can not deny their request
because she knows very well
the healing power of such a circle
and sometimes even the healer
must be healed.

Tears cried
Not only day after day
or minute after minute
but lifetime after lifetime.
Tears for lives lost,
dreams unfulfilled love unrequited.
She weeps not only for herself
but for countless mourners,
for those hungry and forgotten,
for the ones being abused
and for the very earth we inhabit.
Throughout history she has cried,
for miscarriages of justice,
for governments run wild,
for those who hope
things will change and
for those who have lost all hope.
There are many who will not
understand this,
there are many who still sleep
and do not know,
and there are those who, while awake,
feel helpless and lost.
She cries for them too.
Tears fall,

filling oceans of despair,
and of longing,
and of love.
Perhaps one day they will see her,
see who she really is.
But for now, there are only more
tears being cried.

Looking around the room
she sees memories
some happy and some sad.
Memories of vacant land
of building a house
of so many things
they did together
when they were happy.
Memories of loneliness
of being forgotten completely
by the one
she wished she could forget.
She sighs and says "it's time"
time to take a giant leap forward
to a new place
with a new love
to make more happy memories
Happy memories
that will someday
render those old ones
completely healed.

If I ever loved you,
if you ever meant anything to me,
then rest assured
I love you still.
Even if you hurt me
to the point where I
will never speak to you again,
my love for you is still there.
Even if all you ever did was hurt me.
Even if all you ever wanted
was anyone else but me.
My love for you is eternal.
It has probably changed
and grown into something
other than what it was.
But it is still there.
So I need you to know
that when everything is dark
in your life.
When you think you've
gone so wrong no one
will ever love you again.
When you feel completely
unworthy of being loved.
I love you still.

Oh dear girl
with golden hair
you know how I remember,
moving furniture to block your door
and hanging bedspreads across your
window.
How no one knew
what you were going through,
nor would they have believed you
had you told them.
But you were prey to those depraved
who hunted you without ceasing.
And mother wondered
why you ran away
instead of staying like she wanted.
But you had learned at such an early age
that she could not protect you.
So you learned how to protect yourself
through any method needed,
and you've gone through life
always letting go,
instead of finding love completed.
Now dear girl you're growing old
and lamenting broken promises

and all those dreams you left behind
now return with renewed urgency.
What to do but drop the reins
and follow where they take you.
For if dreams still call
they are not dreams
but the destiny that awaits you.

Not a word was spoken between
Beatrix and I
I'd never known a truer friend
nor seen a brighter sky
I knew that she was leaving
A single tear fell from my eye
A little girl, a beloved horse
Beneath that bright blue sky
I felt it should have been raining
or at least cloudy so I could hide
the tears that now streamed
down my face
They would not stay inside
Though not a word was spoken
between Beatrix and I
The moment she lay down to sleep
I knew to stay right by her side
And then we dreamed
of rainbow bridges
underneath that bright blue sky
Then one last ride through dreamland
and her body lay empty by my side
So many years now later and that little
girl is growing old
Yet somehow she still hears them,

forever clear and bold,
all those heartfelt things
you don't have to listen to, to hear
Sounds of a trotting horse
and soft neighing
whispered into
loving ears.
And though not a word was spoken,
between Beatrix and I
She is still here with me underneath
every bright blue sky

A single beam of sunshine
on a snowy day
broke through all the cloudiness
and although it didn't stay
she caught a glimpse of
sunny days and the springtime
soon to come
and her heart, it leapt
maybe just a bit
to think of all those
outside things to be done
So much to do and
so much to plan
Planting, pruning and more
It almost made her run outside
and leave the warm indoors.
But alas the sunbeam left too soon
as suddenly as it had come
leaving her with a cup of tea
and a book to carry on
Still the memory of that speck of sun
stayed warmly in her thoughts
for that last few weeks of winter
will be gone soon enough.

She is tired,
her strength has weakened
Her energy fluctuates
between barely there
and not there at all.
The war she has waged
since the beginning of time
against the darkness and the evil
have taken a toll.
All she wants now is to sleep
so she can return
renewed, refreshed
her strength regained
so she can wage her war again.

Long before the stars
welcomed you home
and the birds sang out your name
our love was real
before dinosaurs roamed the earth,
and when the mountains
had not yet risen
we were us
Throughout history,
as nations rose and fell
and wars were fought
our souls were intertwined
Truthfully
there are times
I am convinced
we were the spark
that ignited
the big bang.
And I love you still.

Somewhere in the world
there is a girl
who tends to the animals
and makes plants grow
she sings to the stars
and writes about her life
knowing very well
most will never read her words.
But she also knows
there will be one
who will read her words
and fall in love
with the spaces in between.

Snow falling
One lone dove sits at a feeder
long since blown empty by the wind,
in a final desperate attempt to eat
it floats to the ground
finding not only food
but shelter from the wind
and the snow at the base of the tree
beneath the feeder.
The wind will end soon enough
leaving a blanket of cold,
wet snow everywhere.
And the loan dove will again
venture out,
knowing sooner or later
the kind woman who lives there
will fill the feeder again.
Cycles repeating almost without notice
in a quiet corner
of Arizona.

If she doesn't know you,
don't expect her just to engage,
she isn't shy, it's just that
she doesn't make small talk
and she isn't interested about
how you feel about the weather,
or who you know
or why you think you're special.
If you want her to open up
you have to speak her language.
She speaks the language of the stars,
communicates with beings
from other worlds and dimensions
and knows of so many things
you refuse to see.
So, ask her about
wild elephants in Thailand,
talk to her about the asteroid belt or
bigfoot.
Talk to her about what's in your heart,
tell her what really matters to you,
what you're afraid of,
what you're proudest of.
Ask her what she likes most
about being human

and what she likes least.
Once you let her see who you are
she will reciprocate.
But be absolutely certain this is what you
want.
She has blown the minds of beings so
much larger than you.

If I ever see you again
I will tell you about how wonderfully
my life has changed.
I will talk about how much
I miss the little things
but that I'm very happy now.
Because you don't deserve
the real me anymore.
Perhaps you never did.
The real me is messy
and deeply feeling
and silly and sometimes sad.
The real me never cared
if you had money
or even a job.
I cared only about you
and I cared about you being happy
and if it took a big job
paying lots of money
to make you happy,
I was ok with it.
But really I wasn't ok with any of it.
Because you changed into someone else.
And I could not abandon myself
in order to keep you in my life.

There's nothing remarkable about them
they're just tiny little gray balls of fluff
no special markings
no grumpy faces
not even a stripe or a spot.
It will be really difficult
for them to find good homes.
For in this day and age
it seems one must be extraordinary
to be loved.
Especially if you are a tiny little
gray ball of fluff
born to a feral mother
who was killed by a tractor.

Sometimes it's all so overwhelming
the pain of the world
that she feels deep within her heart.
Pain that washes over her
like shells on a beach
forever pulling her this way and that
until she's too deep under the waves
to swim
And she waits for that single
positive thought,
that makes her float
to the surface once more
So she can transmute the pain
and finally recover herself
again.

On quiet mornings
she sends love to the world
and healing to those who need it
and peace to those
who live in chaos
and she drinks coffee
and watches the birds
and realizes how very precious
life truly is.
But often her mornings are not quiet
they're filled with
the sounds of animals
wanting breakfast
or to go outside for a morning stroll
and on these mornings she
still sends love to the world
and healing to those who need it
and peace to those
who live in chaos.
For she knows
that on those louder mornings
all of those things
are much more necessary
and important.

It seems to me
that human beings
might just have some things
backwards.
We're told that to enjoy
better days
we need to chase the tears away,
when truly tears
are what is needed
and to fully feel those tears
is to heal the pain
and healing leads
to those better days.

I guess if I were honest here
and I could say what I
should have said,
I'd tell you that I love you first
because that is the truest thing.
Next I'd say that you were wrong
in assuming the things you did
based on those who didn't know me
and in fact, they didn't know you either.
People like drama
and if they can't find it,
they'll create drama themselves,
and then they work hard to
get everyone else to participate
in their play.
But drama isn't truth.
Drama is, at least mostly, destructive.
And we truly had no drama
until they decided to fill your head
with the story they created.
So we lost. No one won.
Except for drama.

She has the heart of an angel,
and often,
the mouth of a sailor.
She's hard to figure out
and if you don't put in the effort
to really get to know her
well, then she will always
be that mysterious
quiet one in the corner.
But if you take your time,
talk to her, really listen
to what she has to say.
She will change your
views about everything.
And if you have the strength
to stay,
she will change your life.

Some days
she writes for hours
never about one single thing
but about this thing
and that.
She pours her soul
into each page
with the hope that someone
will hear her words
and know her soul
and the depths of her pain.
Pain unlike most will ever know.
For it is that pain
that has shaped her
molded her every fiber
and every thought,
for much of this pain remains.
And it is this reason
she flits from thing to thing
to set upon each page,
for if she stuck with one thing
for too long,
she is convinced
pain alone
would set fire to it all.

I remember that Thanksgiving,
that gathering when
I sat on a couch with friends
and you took my picture.
How we'd laughed about it later,
how we both knew someone
beside me
thought you were focused on her.
That picture,
the one you kept in your wallet
for decades
until your death.
The very picture I now hold
in my hands.
I'm so thrilled it meant that
much to you,
I'm thrilled I meant that much to you.
For "we" really never were.
With all the flirting and all
the hugs and all the people
that thought we were together.
But no.
For what they didn't know,
didn't realize,

was that you were neither
left-handed
or a bass player.
And I was blonde.
An inside joke that still lingers
all these years after you left
this planet.
Always reminding me
of how much we were
even though we
never were.

On any given afternoon
when the sun hides behind the clouds
and the wind is stronger
than she likes it to be,
she thinks of those she's lost,
carefully remembering
each tiny thing she can recall.
Of course through the years
she misses each of them a little less,
and the sting of grief
hurts just a bit less.
Still she embraces the sound
of each voice,
their smiles and hugs.
Mostly she misses their laughter.
Sometimes she can still hear it.
Ringing throughout time and space
beyond the veil
finally reaching her ears,
laughing on the wind
stronger than she likes,
when the sun hides behind the clouds
on any given afternoon.

I heard someone say that maybe
friendship has an expiration date
that we don't know about.
But I don't think so,
if we love someone, we love them,
love does not die, it just changes.
Often it changes because
we do things that are
terribly unloving.
So perhaps this person
who thought friendship
had an expiration date
had done something either deliberately
or unintentionally
that was unkind, unloving,
to their friend.
And that friend then
decided out of love for themselves
to change the love for their friend
into the type of love
that is from afar,
the "I'll love you from over here" love
that lasts forever, even though
they do not want you in their life
anymore.

I sat on the ground
beside the grave of an excellent dog.
A dog who would have done
anything for me.
As I sat there, missing this furry soul,
a living, breathing very-much-alive
dog came and sat beside me.
Since he is quite old now
and his hips are sore,
I gently massaged his hip,
he then switched sides so I could do the
same to the other one.
I struggled to my feet and watched
as he struggled to his.
As I walked away I noticed
he'd gone back
to the grave of an excellent dog
as if to say "I've got her now, it's ok."
then he trotted as quickly as his
old body could trot to
catch up with me
finally leaning against my leg
as I stopped to marvel
at the love of an excellent dog.

A soft breeze, a light rain, even a raging
thunderstorm or a sunny day
all remind me of you.
As do still nights filled with stars,
mountains rising to the sky,
and any body of water that
catches my eye.
Truthfully you are everywhere I look,
you are in everything I touch,
and in every song I hear.
There have been times lately
when I have felt you so strongly
I have let myself believe
for a second that you are
still here with me.
Long ago you became my favorite
guardian angel,
long ago your voice was silenced,
and I set your ashes free to be
one with the wind,
the rain and your favorite
raging thunderstorms.
Today I still miss you
as I did that day.
But today I feel

your presence strongly and
I know truly
love does last forever,
and for now,
that will have to be enough.

If you find the girl I used to be,
please just pass her by
because she's not me
and I am not her anymore.
I remember her though,
she was always looking,
searching relentlessly,
for love from others
rather than finding the love
for herself on the inside.
The consummate chameleon,
quickly deducing what each person
wanted her to be,
then becoming it.
Never really knowing herself.
Finally life taught her those lessons,
and while they were devastating
to learn,
learn them she did.
Until she and I
became very different people.
So if you ever run across her again,
know she will not be me.
And you might not like me as myself.

Here's to all the introverts,
the empaths and the misfits.
We simply do not fit in.
Perhaps that's only
because we're here to
make a new world.
A world where people
say what they mean,
and what they feel,
rather than simply talk about the weather,
or last night's game, or each other.
Where it's ok, not to be ok.
And to talk about anything,
or nothing, at all,
but especially to talk about
those things that cause us pain.
A world where it's
completely acceptable
and even encouraged,
to love who you love
and to be exactly who
you want to be,
whether you were born that way or not.
A world where everyone fits in,

where no one feels like an outcast,
or a joke or as
someone born to be made fun of,
or bullied.
For we dream of a world
that puts love first
and above all else.
And what a beautiful world
that will be indeed.

Some days are just difficult,
everything is just heavy
and it hurts to breathe
much less to do anything at all
productive.
Everyone has those days.
Sometimes it isn't that anything is wrong,
it's just that nothing is right.
We aren't where we think we should be,
and we haven't done enough
to prove we are worthy.
On those days it's so important
to remember you are worthy
of whatever you want to be
worthy of.
Give yourself a hug,
or a special treat,
or both.
Know this will pass
and tomorrow likely will not
feel as heavy as today does.
If not tomorrow then the next day.
Change will come,
be here to greet it.

You ask why I hate you,
but that really isn't right
at all.
Truthfully I love you,
so very much,
but we don't belong
in each other's lives.
It isn't because of circumstances,
whatever was done was done.
It is simply because you would only
hurt me,
and I would only hurt you too.
Forever it has been this way,
way back since time began.
We are neither friends
nor enemies,
we are just two beings trying hard
to understand
that it's far better to love
someone dearly from afar
than to engage in needless battles
over the affairs
of broken hearts.

The spirit of a cat
brushes against her leg
with enough force
to let her know he's there.
But she was expecting him,
for every time she sits
in her studio control room
he's there.
As if he's waiting for his chance
to drum or give the guitar a go.
In life he wasn't allowed in there,
but in death she can not keep him out.
So each morning she knows
when she goes to work,
he will show up.
A recording studio softly haunted,
by the ghost
of Mo.

Some people think
love is that feeling in the
beginning of a relationship
that's all tingly and
makes you giggle.
But that's infatuation not love.
Love is understanding
that everyone has scars
and no one is perfect.
Love is being there
when the one you're with
is having a tough day,
or is undertaking a project
way out of their comfort zone.
Love is knowing life comes
with hard times,
with losses
and wins.
Love is being there
when the one you love
needs you.
Love is burying much-loved animals and
sometimes even much-loved people.
Love is being willing to
stay up all night

when the one you are with
needs to stay up and talk.
Love is working things out
rather than just walking away
when things get tough.

If you were anyone else
I would have told you
that things will get better,
that you'll get through it
and that bad times never
last for very long.
If you were anyone else,
I probably would have
given some impromptu speech
about how going through
this stuff will
make you stronger.
But you weren't anyone else,
you were someone I love
more than anyone else,
you were my daughter.
And I know all the horrible
things you've gone through,
and I know how it does appear
that your bad times
have lingered.
And I know if there were anyone
who ever had no use
to be any stronger,
it is you.

So all I could do
was offer a shoulder
to soak up your tears,
tell you how very much
I love you,
and tell you I will listen
to every word you need to say,
for as long as you need to talk.
Because you already knew
this too shall pass.
And you already knew
there is no light
without the dark.
So I did my best
to be a comfort to you.
But right this second
all I can think of
is that my child was hurting
and really nothing I
could ever do
was enough
to keep that pain
from hitting
your heart.

He said I write
from my soul
and he didn't understand
how anyone could
bare their soul in that way.
For years now I've thought
about those words he said,
for he said them as if it were
to be taken as some sort of insult.
I write how I write.
That's it.
And if I leave pieces of my soul
upon page after page,
then so be it.
He wouldn't be there
to clean up
those pieces
anyway.

How I admire her courage,
being the smallest
of the pack
yet forcefully controlling
everyone's actions,
intensely expressing herself
all the while skillfully
dodging the nips
of the largest among them.
I watch her closely
so she isn't hurt,
yet it is the largest
who has a bloody nose.
Charlotte, however do you do it?
This tiny chihuahua brute
of a dog.

She sits outside
and watches the birds
and drinks coffee.
A jack rabbit races by
chased by a dog,
and the pond fountain turns on,
startling a frog
who lets out a loud croak.
The trees are showing
signs of spring,
but she is not fooled,
for she's seen snow here
in May
and it is only March.
Looking around
she sees so many things,
things to be done
and she knows
she can not
do them by herself.
She shrugs it off,
knowing she will do her best
and that
will have to be enough.

As she settles in to her favorite
rocking chair on the porch,
takes another sip of coffee
and waits for spring.

She treats the animals as people,
for they are, after all,
sentient beings.
This statement brings forth
a conversation in the room
of beginning spirituality students.
What does it really mean
to be a sentient being?
All we need to do
is pay attention
to the creatures in nature
to realize we all feel,
we all love
and each of us is only
trying to survive.
Even flowers will feel
the sun's warmth
and move to face it.
So then don't we live
in a sentient world?
"Of course we do"
says one girl
who has not uttered a word
until now.
And we all agree

that if we all feel love,
if even the animals and plants
feel things,
if we are all sentient beings
then we should all be
treating each other
a lot better than we are.

She feels the energy
of someone new,
someone who is coming into her life
like a great storm.
And she will pretend
not to see his demons
even though she will not
forget they are there.
Two opposites of character,
yet amazingly,
exactly the same.
So she will pretend
she doesn't see them
until the time comes
for them to join forces
and fight demons
together.

Life is often brutal
and dark, and unforgiving.
It's true that whatever it is
that you count on the most
will likely fail you
exactly when you need it.
So know,
you who are
going through
a dark night of the soul,
you are not alone.
Understand earth school is hard,
and in order to grow your soul
you will need courage
and faith.
Courage to face the darkness
within you.
And faith to believe with all you are
and with everything you
ever will be,
that you will get through this
and you will feel the sun
and marvel at it's light
again.

Sometimes
she feels as if
she's in a state of
suspended animation,
watching time
go speeding by
unable to do anything
of importance.
Then again she knows
that time is only
a construct of man,
so maybe in the watching
she is learning more than
she realizes.
And that is an awfully
important thing
to do.

He noticed
one of her legs is
slightly shorter than the other,
and he deduced
that's why her hips
are always bothering her.
And from there
he realized her back
must also be sore,
so he put his hand
ever so gently
on the small of her back
and asked her
if that's where it hurt.
All of this
within the first five minutes
of meeting.
And it scared her to think
that the man
she prayed for
might just
be real.

Why is it always a door?
People say
when one door shuts
another opens
like doors are the only openings
available in buildings
of any kind.
Why not a window?
At least in most buildings
windows open and shut
just as doors do.
These are the things
that keep her up
most nights.
Things she really
doesn't mind thinking about.
For these things are far better
to ponder
than darker things.
Silly human-created scenarios
inhabiting her mind
as she tries
to sleep.

A cool, soft breeze
flows down from the mountains
just in time
to dry the sweat
from her forehead.
She lifts her head
from the raspberry bush
she just split into three
just in time to catch
not only the breeze
but the pair of hawks
soaring high above
riding the thermal winds.
"Life is good" she said
apparently to the nearby cat
or to the breeze itself,
knowing it really didn't matter
which of them she spoke to,
for the spirits of the land
heard her voice
and were pleased.

It had never occurred to him
that she'd had a life
before him.
But in fact,
she'd lived enough
to fill several lives
to the brim,
way before he ever
entered her life.
She didn't care that he'd
never considered
who she was before him.
In fact, she sort of liked it.
Until the day
when he realized
she'd lived at least
three lifetimes in one.
It was then he began
to treat her differently
as if she were something
terribly broken
that could never
be put back together
again.

A long time ago
she remembered their past lives,
and who he was before.
She remembered a great love,
cut short by war,
and the grief that followed.
A while ago
she recognized him,
as he is in this life.
And she just could not fathom
how on earth
their paths would cross.
Yet angels and guides say
he is coming soon
into her life,
this life, right now,
in this dimension.
And she remembers the grief
from before
and she is just not
absolutely certain
that she will survive
that grief again.

A raven caws
just to say hello
and say they're back
now that it's not so cold
So she goes outside
to welcome back her friends
because she knows
this friendship has no end
for in saving one,
she saved them all
and three generations later
they're back to caw
a "hello friend
we have returned
and you will never lack
for big, black birds."

Hours later
and she's still waiting,
for the knock at the door
that announces the person
who said he'd be there at noon
to help her.
For years it's been this way,
she asks for help,
begs for help,
finally someone will say
"of course I'll help,
why didn't you ask sooner?"
only to leave her waiting
and waiting
putting her life on hold
so that someone can finally
stop by and do nothing
after saying
he'd be there at noon
to get everything done.

She has a wicked sense of humor
and it's been said that
she could give you directions
straight to hell
and you'd be grateful for her time.
But she isn't difficult,
at least not like they say.
She simply does not belong
where she is currently at.
She's outgrown it,
and while it's still very important
and very close to her heart,
she's ready to leave.
So she looks for her chance,
and waits for the one she knows
is coming soon,
the one with scars that match her own,
both physical and not.
Then she'll literally drive off
into the sunset
to a new life in a new place
a little more fitting
for one like herself.

Today
has not been
a very good day.
In fact it's been
quite awful.
So since it appears
all is lost,
let's have waffles for dinner
and perhaps red wine
and chocolate for dessert.
Because since it hasn't been
a good day
we should certainly end it
in the best possible manner.

When I said that
I loved you,
when I wrote poems to you,
saying how much you meant to me,
did you not believe me?
When I stood
on that beach
professing my love forever,
saying how I'd always be there
for you,
did you not listen?
Somewhere along the way
you forgot all about me,
you forgot I existed,
that I was even in your life.
At some point you began to listen
to other people's opinions
and their problems, and their drama
and your own insecurities
and you stopped communicating with me.
And those people with their problems,
and their drama and your own
insecurities.
Became more important to you,
than I was.

She sat under an apple tree
in dappled light
in early spring.
And she watched the bees
swarming around
the first blossoms
of the season.
And her mind wandered
back in time
to another day
in early spring.
She had planted this tree
when it was very small
and he'd laughed at her,
he said she'd never
get a tree from that stick,
much less an apple.
Yet in the years since he'd been gone,
she'd eaten many apples
and baked many pies
And she hoped he was happy
and well
then she continued watching bees
swarm around the first blossoms
of the season.

Sometimes we get bogged down
in thoughts about things
we did wrong
or that the other person did wrong.
And we begin to believe
things will never go right
and we'll never be happy.
But here's the thing.
Sometimes people are like plants
who just have to be fertilized
with a lot of crap
in order to grow.

What if I told you
that I'd felt your energy
long before we met?
If I said that I'd
seen you in a dream
or on the astral plane?
Would you believe me?
Would you want to hang out
and learn more?
Would you simply say
"yes, I have seen you there
and I too have felt your energy."
Or would you look at me
like I'm just another crazy person
unattached to reality
and turn away?
I wonder if I should even
mention any of this.
For one thing I do not need
is another person
who does not believe.

She's not a fan of games,
she doesn't care for small talk
and she is her most uncomfortable
when being made the center
of attention.
She's entirely complicated
in her simplicity,
believing in beings from space,
big foot, fairies and of course
all manner of things paranormal.
She's amazingly loyal
and attentive
to those she loves
and craves nothing so much
as to be held and caressed
by one who will not only
join her in her oddness
but relish it's freedom.

When you find yourself,
and you will,
in utter turmoil
and disdain for life.
I hope you remember
that truly we are all one.
And anything any one of us feels
is felt throughout all of us.
So know first
that you are not alone
in your loneliness.
And whatever it is that you feel,
well that feeling has been felt
many times before
by so many of us.
So please give yourself some time,
remember that change is constant
and that your life and
your circumstances will change.
I hope you can give yourself
a hug, or a pat on the back
for each day you continue,
until that beautiful day
when changes does come
into your life.

Remembering the rain,
and why does it always
seem to rain at funerals
and other sad times?
But I do remember the rain,
it was different that day,
the day we spread your ashes
and said our goodbyes.
There were not many of us,
so many hateful and bigoted
family members decided
not to attend.
But that was ok because those
who loved you most were there.
And honestly we never liked them
anyway.
But the rain was softer than usual,
it seemed kinder,
more compassionate.
It was as if the angels in heaven
felt our loss
and cried with us.
And that's what we all agreed.
Those of us who were there in the rain.
For you.

She said she wasn't going
to write today,
yet here she was, writing away,
writing about nothing
and yet everything.
Spilling her soul on to paper
as if it were the
most important thing
anyone could do.
A smile gradually filled her face
as she realized how
she'd loved to read
her grandmother's journals
after she'd transitioned
and she realized that perhaps,
just perhaps,
it truly was the most important thing,
anyone could do.
We never know who our words might
touch,
or how much those words might mean,
to someone in the future
who only got to know us
through our words.
So she continued writing away.

It's important
to never stop playing,
for in imagination
we lay the groundwork
for the life we
want to live.
This she had said
as a small lizard
crawled up
and down
her arm,
while on the ground
a cat
waited to pounce.
She gently placed
the lizard
on a nearby tree
and told the cat
that the cycles of life
would have to wait
another day.

If it weren't for daydreams
I'd have no life at all
for it has been those
mindless wanderings
through the ethers
that have proved to me
exactly who I am
and those things in life
that are most important
for me to experience
and for me to love.

At this place in her life,
she laughs a lot
remembering the girl she was
and the woman she's become.
She laughs at so many things
no one knows,
and truthfully no one will
ever know
if she has her way about it.
She laughs at things
she once cried about.
At all those things she once wanted
and at how trivial they
all seem now.
At this place in her life,
she laughs,
sometimes at nothing in particular
and other times at
the whole of it.
Truly, she's learned
to laugh at it all.

Know that your tears
are you healing
Know that sad days
mean better ones are ahead
Know always that
you are never alone
and there's always
someone who cares,
even if you must search
to find them.
Know that whatever
you are going through
is only temporary.
Finally you absolutely
must believe you
are here for a reason
and the world
needs you,
for only you can do
the things you must do
and whatever that is,
it is vital to
all of us.

Oh how I remember
that tiny white foot,
sticking out the window
as she pulled up,
saying only that
she'd found someone
who needed me.
Of course you were yet
another mutt-puppy,
with your white foot,
and black and tan body
with a white chest
with a perfect alien face on it.
I never fell harder or quicker
for anything ever than
I did with you.
Now that tiny white foot is huge,
and you grew so much more
than I ever thought you would,
and now that you're old
you have trouble walking,
or standing for very long,
and your eyesight is dimming
and I'm quite certain
your hearing is pretty much gone.

But each time I sit on the couch or
anywhere really,
you still reach out to me
with that once tiny white foot
as if to say you love me so,
but your time is
growing short.
And I know that. I do.
So I watch and listen
for you to tell me
when it's time.
And I so hope you decide
to just take a long nap
and not wake up.
But if you need my help,
know I'll be there
holding that white foot
the whole time.
Until you're at peace
across the rainbow bridge.

She's asked for help
so many times
she will not ask again
for all it does it prove to her
she really has no friends.
Oh they say
"all you have to do is call"
but no one is ever there
oh they're just all so busy
or is it they don't care.
So things just don't get done
at least not the way they did before
so those rooms she can not muster
she will just close the door.
And next time that they tell her
all she needs to do is call
she won't even bother
to respond
they've proven their
unreliability
she's better talking to the wall.

I remember days
when you would call
and I would immediately
drop whatever I was doing,
even if what I was doing
was something terribly important.
I was so desperate for a friend,
for someone, literally anyone,
to care about me that I
abandoned myself entirely
for that chance.
But you, you were never my friend.
Talking behind my back
as you did.
Making sure I had no other
"friend" than you.
Eventually getting between
me and my husband even.
Years after I cut you from my life
I'm still hearing from people
I never knew cared.
But they had cared,
they still do.
It was you who never really did.

I'm sure one day
this will all make sense,
I have to believe that.
Otherwise all of this
would have been for nothing
and I simply can't tolerate
that thought.
So each day I recover
pieces of myself
that have been broken
and ripped apart
from my soul.
And I truly believe
one day I will look back
at all the horrible events
of my life,
and they will have become
less horrible
causing me to smile.

To say that she loves animals
is to say you require
oxygen to breathe.
For without them
she surely would have
been dead for some time now.
Few could ever understand
how they've saved her life
time and time again.
Through illness
and disease and heartbreak,
oh so much of these.
Always they've been there
with love and compassion
and caring.
People,
well people,
not so much.

No, she isn't shy.
But she hates small talk
and parties,
well, really gatherings of any kind.
She's quiet,
always the observer
usually in a corner somewhere.
You can rest assured
if she opens her mouth
she truly has something to say.
And whatever that is,
you're going to
want to hear it.

Please find me
and I will tell you stories
of places and of beings
and of other things
you never knew existed.
Please find me
and I will let you know
how very much
I love the mountains
and the ocean.
Please find me
if you are sad,
and I will listen to every tear
until you are happy
again.
Please find me
and I will keep you company
for the rest of your life,
for this life and for all
of eternity.
Just.
Please.
Find me.

The bumper sticker said
"Live your bliss."
And while she appreciated
the sentiment very much,
she couldn't help but wonder
what bliss they were referring to.
As is normally the case
her first thought went to the animals,
certainly her bliss was there,
right?
But the lives of animals are usually
not entirely blissful
so perhaps this sticker meant
something else.
So she wondered about the earth, the
plants, the sky, the oceans, the
mountains...maybe bliss was there.
And truly she did find bliss was present
in each of those.
Somehow though, she didn't think this
was the sticker's intention.

So she thought of writing, something that
definitely was blissful most of the time,
but not always.
In face every single thing she thought of
could not be considered blissful
all of the time.
Then is occurred to her this was
the entire point.
To find bliss in each and every thing
we do in each moment.
Finally, she liked
her conclusion.

There are times
when she receives messages
from the other side of the veil
for people on this side,
but she doesn't know who
the message is for.
Other times it's entirely
clear and she is certain
who needs the message
she receives.
A gift in progress
she thinks.
Though she knows
eventually it will all
be sorted out
and each recipient
will receive the message
they are ready
to receive.

When you are in
a very dark place
and you just can't see the light,
sit with it,
in the dark,
for as long as it takes
until you can see
the light of your own soul.
Only then will the clouds part
leaving you in the
light again.

Patience?
Never have I been
a particularly patient person.
No, in fact I've been known
to be a particularly
impatient one.
Still, here is someone
in front of me saying anytime
she starts to get frustrated
she thinks of me and my patience
with things.
Does she not know me?
Then she talks of my patience
with a very frightened rescue dog.
And of how I spent hours outside
on cold, rainy night trying
to coax a lost, feral kitten
out of a tree.
And I get it.
Maybe it's simply
that I reserve patience
for only those things that
matter most.

She gets tired, sometimes,
of the weirdness
that is her life.
Those deceased for decades
or even hundreds of years,
just popping in to see
what she's doing.
Messages for others
being given from loved ones
on the other side of the veil.
Even animals who have
transitioned make their
appearances.
On occasion, even a being
from another world stops by.
Right when she's about to scream
"leave me alone"
one of them thanks her
profusely,
for allowing them to say their peace.
Then she realizes how very lucky
she is to have this life, and this gift,
that sometimes makes her very tired
of the weirdness.

It's amazing how they find her,
those animals who just show up
at her door.
But find her they do, they always have.
She tells people it's her animal
magnetism and it may well be,
for she was that kid who really did get
followed home by strays.
As an adult those strays even
included several people.
All needing her for something
whether food, or a place to sleep,
or as someone they could use for a while.
These days she's back to stray
animals though.
And she's often heard saying
"If I ever find that animal who is
giving out road maps to my house
they're going to be in big trouble."
But everyone knows she's not
going to change,
for that animal magnetism is stronger
than ever.
And her heart won't let her
turn them away.

The worry game is one
you will never win.
In fact worry will make you lose
time and time again.
Everything is energy and worry
isn't one you want to increase.
Better instead to focus your
attention on that energy
you want to multiply.
I know that is much easier
to say than to do,
but one thing I've found
that makes it just a bit easier
is to pay attention to your thoughts.
When you find yourself worrying,
thank the worry for showing you
that you need to change your focus.
With practice you will notice
better things coming into your life
probably including that very thing you
were so worried about.

She's moved a lot in her life,
not always because
she wanted to move,
but because circumstances
meant it was unavoidable.
She'd thought she'd found her
forever home.
But no, she's been where she is
for too long now.
And in looking back over her life
and her previous moves,
she realizes something she'd never
before considered.
She really isn't looking for a place
or a building,
she's truly searching for
the man who feels like home.

If I were to tell you who I truly am,
who I've been
and who I will never be again,
what would you do?
Would you stand with me in the shadows
of all those dark yesterdays?
Or would you decide
I'm just too much to handle?
I admit I am a lot to handle.
But with all the deep feelings,
the eloquent speeches about nothing,
lasting long into the night,
the pain over the injustices
and abuses of the world.
I have a heart that loves deeper
than any ocean and harder
than any mountain.
And I would give it freely and forever
If only I could find the man
strong enough to feel all these things
with me.
And who is not afraid of feeling them,
because he has made friends with all his
dark yesterdays and
deep feelings are his forte.

People are not being helpful when they
say "let it go" or "whatever you think
about is what you are creating" simply
because there is no explanation.
So to let something go
is simply to notice your thoughts
and when you have one you really don't
want or one that seems to just bring up
the past, change your mind.
It's true that we create our own realities
and if your current one is
not where you want to be.
You have the power to create the one you
want. Really. You do.
Focus on how you want to feel in life
instead of how you do feel. That's how
you begin.
Then take time each day to focus on how
it is you want to feel and what it is you
really want in your life.
Eventually you will find you
have created that feeling and it has
become the way you feel all the time.

When you reach this point it is likely
those things have followed your feelings
into your life.
Or perhaps you've decided
these are truly not things
you really wanted.

If we could just see each other
through the eyes of love
how much more tolerant
we would all become.
If you could just see me
the way that I see you
how much more love and kindness
would ensue.
Love is the answer
and it has always been
for with love humanity flies higher
and wars would forever end.
If we could just love each other
the way we love ourselves
we'd each have all we need
and we'd want for nothing else.

Please smile
you who are going
through a hard time,
you who haven't left your house
in weeks,
you who have stopped eating
healthy meals.
Maybe you are drinking too much
these days
and maybe you've even stopped
talking to friends and family.
I need to ask you to do something,
not for me, for yourself.
Please take a minute, or
even a second
and face yourself in a mirror,
look yourself in the eyes,
and smile.
I know it won't make you feel better
immediately,
but doing this every time you
think of it,
will allow those mirror smiles
to become real ones.
Please, just smile.

I remember the drive-in,
I remember the station wagon
and the child's potty-chair in the back.
It was dark and I'd been drinking soda,
and I asked my mother
to walk me to the bathroom.
The fit he threw
scared both of us.
And he wasn't in our lives
long after that,
but still
it was decades before I asked
to use a bathroom again.
Scars remembered
under the full moon of healing
and transmutation
and forgiveness
and love.

She's just a girl
Dancing barefoot, outside,
alone, under the stars
She's just a girl who has known intense
trauma and abuse in her life
She's known those she loved
literally try to kill her,
or move out while she was at work,
or cheat after becoming
jealous and bitter as she tried
to make life better for both of them.
She's just a girl who has known the
agony of conceiving a child
who would not live,
and the grief of surviving the deaths of
both a best friend and a brother
among many others
She's just girl with more scars on her
body than most, either from injury
or surgeries.
She's seen the worst that life can offer.
Still, she's just a girl who works
constantly to make life better for animals.

She dreams of establishing a local
healthy food bank because there are just
too many hungry people.
She's just a girl who in spite of the way
life has treated her still believes most
people are good
and life is worth living.
There are days when she speaks to more
dead people than living ones
and she counts angels
and animals among her best friends.
To you she might seem unique,
different or weird.
She might even seem
somehow selfless or heroic.
But to her
She's just a girl
Dancing barefoot,
outside,
alone,
under the stars

I truly believe magic is real,
however there is no pill you can take,
meditation you can do or
frog you can kiss
that will make all your dreams come true,
if you are only doing these things
because someone told you
that you should do them.
No one can give you your dreams.
No one else can tell you what makes
your heart sing.
Only you really know who you are,
so listen to your heart.
A good teacher never simply gives
the student the answers,
but helps each student find those
answers for themselves.

It is hoped that by baring my soul
I have helped you more deeply connect
with your own.
This journey we are all on,
this earth school, is a difficult one.
Remember that love is
always the answer.

Other books by Kellie Fitzgerald include:

When on the Road to Enlightenment,
Don't Forget to Take out the Trash

Lyrics and Lines from Another Life

Resilient

Beyond the Loss

Laehli & the Elephants, Making Friends

Laehli & the Elephants, The Big Search

Laehli & the Elephants, Smoke